JASON ROBERTS

Empty-handed Odin

This book is dedicated to the people.
You are now blessed with the path of the empty-hand.
Survive, thrive, and enjoy your life.

Contents

Disclaimer

This book is for informational purposes only. The author is not responsible for anything that might occur to anyone working with fire,water, or electricity. The processes and builds in this book pose a risk to your health and safety, and should only be done by trained professionals. Use extreme caution when working with electricity and fire. The author is not a licensed professional in any of these fields or topics and is only providing information. Neither the author nor the publisher shall be held liable or responsible for any loss or damage allegedly arising from any suggestion or information contained in this book. Proceed with extreme caution.

1

Introduction

Empty-handed Odin wields the power of the gods within him. He is lightning, thunder, fire, rain, and wind incarnate. All these nature powers can be manifested through him into this physical dimension by channeling the knowledge and understanding of these forces from his mind, through his body, and out of his empty hands. He is pure power potential, manifested in its human form.

This book is about the path of the empty-hand. Primitive survival skills for the modern world. I will teach you how to manifest electricity from the sun, wind, and magnets without any starting tools or supplies. I will also teach you about water filtration and blacksmithing without any tools to start with. After reading this book you will be able to walk into any house with empty hands, and manifest electricity, clean water, and fire for infrastructure survival. This book is tailored for the average person who may have no prior knowledge, skills, tools, preps, or equipment. One day they may find themselves in a natural disaster survival situation. This book will help them build things for survival and have a higher quality of life while waiting for utility companies to get everything working again.

First I will share with you how and why I put this book together. One day I was thinking about natural disasters like tornadoes, hurricanes, ice storms, earthquakes, meteors, and solar storms. I know that these events could be devastating for the people involved in them. I also know that if it happened on a large scale, it might be hard for utility companies and agencies to get everything back online very quickly. Some people might have to "rough it" a while. I then asked myself, "What could I do to help?" "How can I prepare us for this?" I realized that I don't have the knowledge, time, and resources to help many people. So I set out to study, research, and learn as much as I could in the areas of infrastructure. Electricity, heat, crafting tools and clean water. I realized that buying all of the stuff needed for every household involved in a disaster would be far to expensive for myself and others. Plus if the people don't already have the items needed, It would be very hard to get them since there may not be electricity for computers, no internet or phone service, and no stores open to buy the stuff. See our dilemma? At that point I realized that all water treatment, electricity, heating, and cooking will all have to be improvised with what is on hand at the local level. I also realized that the best way to help struggling people on a massive nationwide scale, is to take all of the things that I learned, and put together the simplest, easiest, most basic way to achieve survival with no prior knowledge or skill, all inside a small book that can fit in a pocket. So here is that book. I give you, "Empty-handed Odin".

2

Rain

Empty-handed Odin can take the rain and make it clean and pure again. Water purification and filtration. I will show several ways of making just about any water from any source safe to drink. I will even show a way to treat irradiated water in case you live near a power plant that has a meltdown in the future. As you already know, we will be using the empty handed path and assuming you have no knowledge on the subject and no starting tools or supplies.

First step in getting people clean water is to find a decent starter supply source. Moving bodies of water like creeks, streams, and rivers will work great. Ponds and lakes are second choice.

Straining and filtering the water is important before you boil, distill, or chemically treat the water. The simplest and easiest way to strain water is to run it through a cloth sock or clothing item. You can do this several times using a new clean cloth each time. After that step, you want to pass it through several different things to help filter it even more. In this chapter I will show the design for what I call the "Empty-handed Odin's Six

Pack Stack". It is a simple homemade water filtration device made out of empty 2 liter bottles and stuff found in or near every home. It is made by cutting the top of the 2 liter bottles off where the sides even out. Then stick one 2 liter inside the next making a stack. Use a sewing needle or a small nail to put holes in the bottom of each 2 liter. Put a sponge or cloth at the bottom of each 2 liter bottle for extra filtration, separation, and to keep the holes from getting clogged.

Water Filtration - 6 Pack Stack

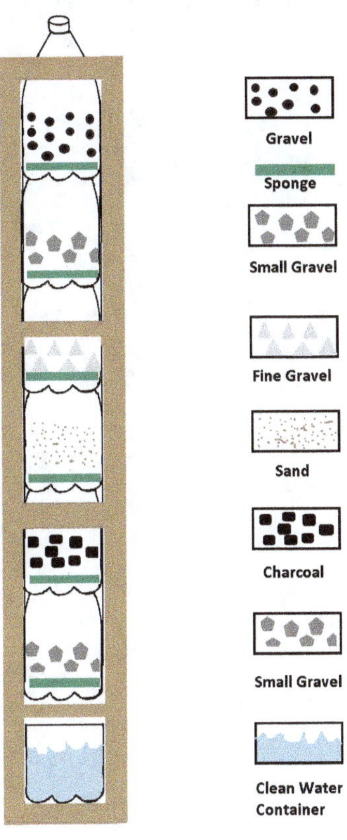

Gravel, fine gravel, activated charcoal, and sand. You can leave out the activated charcoal if you don't want to make any, but you must boil or solar distill the water first for it to be safe. If the water in question has the potential of being irradiated, only using a solar still will make it safe. A solar still can be as simple as a hole in the ground with a plastic bag over it.

Solar Still for Distillation

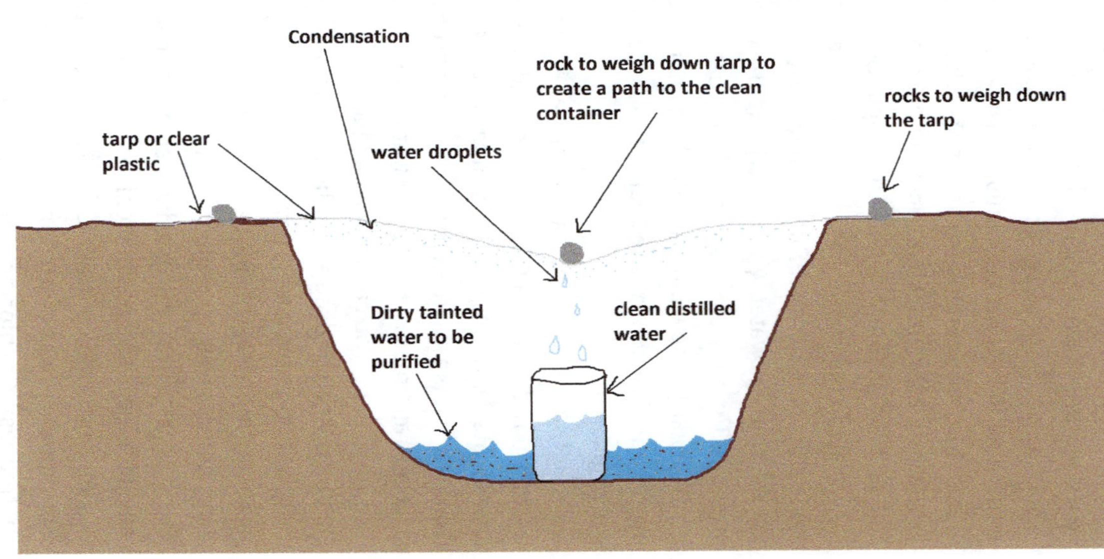

Solar Still

7

This still can also turn salt water into freshwater. The salt will be left at the bottom if you need it.

Boiling water is pretty self explanatory. Start a fire under something to heat the container. When you see water bubbles of high intensity coming to the surface, the water has reached 212 degrees Fahrenheit. Let it boil for 3 more minutes. Cover it and let it cool before you pour it into your Odin's six pack stack.

Activated charcoal is used in most modern professionally made store bought water filters. They use it because it removes toxins from the water without striping the water of salts and minerals. I'm a big fan of activated charcoal, so I will teach you how to make your own. In the "Fire" chapter I teach you how to make your own homemade charcoal, so reference that before you begin.

We will start with homemade charcoal. We start by crushing it into a powder. We take the powder and mix in one to three ingredients depending on what you can find. Calcium chloride is "road salt". It is a salt like compound that is used as a de-icer for sidewalks and roads. If you don't want to use it, or want a more "organic" item, you can instead add lemon juice and vinegar. Pickle juice can be used as a substitute as well. Add enough of the liquids to your charcoal powder to create a paste. Spread this paste out onto a tray, baking pan, or piece of metal and cook it to about 400 degrees Fahrenheit and cook out all of the moisture. Once it is dry and cooled, you have activated charcoal. Now you can add some activated charcoal to your Odin's Six Pack Stack.

I will now explain chemically treating water. The most common disinfectant used in public water systems that you can find easily is chlorine. Chlorine is in what many refer to as bleach. Sodium hypochlorite is the active ingredient in bleach. It's not the natural element chlorine but a mix of many elements almost like chlorine. It will be the easiest thing for you to find, so that is what you will use. The E.P.A. recommends adding 8 drops of bleach to each gallon of water. If you are filling up recycled and cleaned 2 liter bottles, add 4 drops to each bottle. Iodine can also be used to treat water. It is most commonly found in medicine cabinets and first aid kits for disinfecting wounds and abrasions. There are a lot of varieties and purity ranges, so I can't really give you an exact ratio. The E.P.A. recommends that if the tincture of iodine is 2% strength, add 5 drops to each liter of water. That makes 10 drops for a 2 liter bottle, and 18 drops for a gallon jug.

The easiest and best way I have found to save and store water for free is using 2 liter bottles. I buy beverages that come in 2 liter plastic instead of aluminum, I rinse them out after use, and I refill them with tap water. I also add 1 drop of bleach to them for safer long term storage. Do that and you will have a nice amount of emergency water pretty quickly. Some people like old milk jugs, but I don't think they are great for long term for many reasons,but if its all you have for free, wash and rinse them thoroughly and it would work. Add 2 drops of bleach to each gallon jug.

For the adventurous and mechanically inclined, I want to add that a good water pump can be found in an old washing machine. Hook it up to some tubing or pvc pipe going into a water supply, and you could pump water into something easier and faster on a large scale to take with you for later treatment. If you have to do this, it means there are several people without clean water, so it is polite to have enough water treated to share with others.

Now you have many ways to treat water. In the event of a real bad water scenario, I recommend distilling, then boiling, then run it through your 6 pack stack filter, then add some bleach.

That should handle some of the nastiest water you could ever find. Let Empty-handed Odin quench you thirst. Cheers!

3

Fire

Empty-handed Odin has the fire of the gods. This chapter is about empty-handed primitive blacksmithing, metalurgy, and heat creation for the modern world.

Today in modern society, we have an easy life of convenience. We have factories that make us cheap tools and items that we can buy at stores and online. Few people could make their own tools if needed in a survival situation. This section is for those people, but also to ensure this ancient art and craft lives on for future generations.

The art of blacksmithing can be explained very simply. You get a fire hot enough to heat iron so you can bend and shape it. There are a lot of ways to achieve this, but I'm going to explain the most basic empty handed way, and then one simple but upgraded way which can be used for metallurgy as well.

The first method is done using a fire. Burn some wood until you have a good amount of hot coals, get all of the coals together and place your steel on top or inside the coal pile. Be sure you can get it out safely without getting burned or disturbing the fire. Once the metal is red hot, pull it out and quickly hit it to desired shape. You won't have long before it cools and you have to put it back in the coals. Keep repeating this process until your satisfied with your item. There are two more possible steps you can do after this, but it is unnecessary for most primitive items your gonna be making. The other two steps are quenching and tempering. I will explain those in more detail later.

The second method of blacksmithing I want to explain is the charcoal forge. It is my favorite method and with enough practice, you can achieve professional results with it. It is very simple to create with common household items.

The first thing we need for our charcoal forge is charcoal. We will make our charcoal out of wood. The basic scientific explanation of charcoal is that it is wood undergone a chemical change. By burning wood with no air flow, meaning oxygen can't oxidize the carbon inside the wood. The moisture inside the wood is also evaporated and pulled out of the wood, leaving just carbon. (Don't use building lumber unless no other option because of contaminants, chemicals, and toxic vapors)

The easiest and simplest way to do this is to gather up a pile of dead wood and old dried branches. Nothing too large. Dig a hole in the ground that can hold all of your wood. Build a nice fire and make sure all wood is burning and red hot. Once this is achieved, stir it so height of wood and coals are about the same. Now cover the hole with dirt to smother the fire. Make sure to put several inches of dirt on the fire at least. Let the hole and wood cool overnight. Go back to the hole and dig it up 24 hrs later. You will find that your burning wood and coals have turned into charcoal. Gather all of the usable charcoal in a container or sack and store it in a dry place until its time to use it. This primitive method only produces good usable charcoal at a rate of 50% - 75% burnt wood to charcoal output ratio. This is fine for emergencies and small applications, but if you plan to start making knives, and tools for trading, I'll explain a better way. I call it the barrel method.

The barrel method requires a large steel drum, a steel container with a lid, or any material that won't melt. An aluminum fire ring covered with something would work too. Making charcoal in these items is the same procedure. Load it with medium sized wood. Get the fire blazing and ensure even the bottom section of the barrel is on fire too. Put a lid or cover on it to keep air from getting inside. Let it sit about 24 hours to cool and do its chemical transformation. Then open it and you've got yourself a lot of charcoal.

Building the charcoal forge is pretty simple. It only consists of three items. A containment ring, a pipe for air, and a fan. An old steel tire rim works well for the containment forge. Put a steel pipe under one side of the rim going inside the rim. Hook up a small fan on the other end of the pipe to force air into it. This causes the fire and coals to burn hotter.

Tire Rim Forge

You can use any type of fan and run it with a battery or solar panel. It's not necessary, but helps get the steel hotter, faster. You could blow the fire with your own air, fan it with something, or even make a bellow.

Anvils, surfaces, and hammers. Having a hard, flat surface to hammer your metal out is important. You probably wont be able to get an anvil, so just find a flat piece of steel. The thicker, the better. If you are out in the wilderness or can't find flat steel, you could use a thick flat rock. You might break several rocks, but you will get your tools made. That brings me to hammers, I hope you can round up a small sledge hammer or construction hammer, but if not, you can fabricate one. Get two pieces of steel and weld them together using a 12v car battery as a welder.(battery welding is explained in detail in my chapter called Thunder) If you can't find a hammer, or craft one, you could always use a steel pipe if you keep the angle flat when hitting the metal. If all else fails, you can use a big strong rock.

In this next section I will go over three aspects that will take your primitive blacksmithy skills up to a higher quality of product that could rival many of the mass produced items we have now. Annealing, quenching, and tempering. With the understanding of these three processes, with the correct steel choice, and the charcoal forge, I have made tools that could hit other tools and cut them without damaging my tool. You could make a survival knife that can even split wood, but maintain a sharp enough edge to clean fish and animals. These techniques will help you make a high quality tool.

Annealing is the process of heating a metal to red hot uniformly then it being slowly cooled. What this does is make the metal easier to work with. It softens it. Average temperature for annealing most steel alloys is around 1500 F . You can achieve this with a campfire. Build a fire, once you have some coals, throw in your steel. Keep the fire going for a couple hours, then let the fire die out naturally. When you wake up the next morning, carefully remove your steel from the coals and place them outside the fire pit to continue to slowly cool. Once they are room or outside temperature, the annealing process is complete and the steel is soft and ready for blacksmithing. I want to explain why annealing is so important. In this book, I keep the theme of "the empty handed path". This means using different items you can find and salvage to create what you need. Most of the steel items that you will find in the modern world have gone through a hardening and tempering process. If you don't anneal them(make them soft again) they will be hard to hammer and shape.

I will next go into steel selection. There are many types and choices, but I will go into detail about what is referred to as "high carbon steel". You can find it in older car parts and old antique tools. If it looks old and you see rust on it, it probably means that it is steel with a high carbon ratio in it. My most favorite and first round draft pick is an antique file. These tools were specifically made and engineered to cut and shape wood and metal. The best tools I have ever made were from old antique files. (Don't use newer files though, their only case hardened and junk in my opinion for re-tooling) Another good source for high carbon steel is leaf springs in older vehicles. Old chains and old antique tools like hammer heads, chisels, and saw blades contain high carbon steel.

Quenching is the next topic I'm going to discuss. It is basically a hardening process. You heat the metal above its re-crystallization temperature (approximately 1500 F and orange yellow in heat color range) and then you rapidly cool it by dipping it in oil. By cooling the steel almost immediately, it raises the strength and hardness of the steel. I personally like motor oil for this. It's a good way to use your old oil from motor oil changes from your car. You could use water if that is all you have available, but doing so could make the steel too brittle so I advise against it. (If in emergency outdoors situation, and water quenching, put dirt or clay on the back 75 % of the blade so you only harden the sharp blade edge.) Another thing to note is that if you are quenching a knife or tool that is to be sharpened later, only quench or dip the part of the steel that will have the sharpened edge. Doing this will give you a very strong and hardened edge that will maintain its sharpness after extensive use. The other important and most overlooked aspect of "edge quenching" is the fact that not quenching the other 75% of the steel will leave it softer and less likely to break. This is important in striking tools. Some professionals like the ancient samurai sword makers, even went as far as to cover the back 75% of the blade with clay to keep that part from getting too hot and quenched in the process. This makes for a springy, strong, resilient knife, but a hardened sharp edge. If you don't have clay available, you could use dirt or wet moss. Clay is used for its heat resistant properties, but you can improvise.

So as you can see, quenching is a scientific process for creating a high performance tool. I just made it simple for you to understand and replicate. Heat steel to orange hot, dip 25% of the steel in motor oil. Consider it quenched. Your tool is ready for final sharpening and polishing.

Quenching a Tool

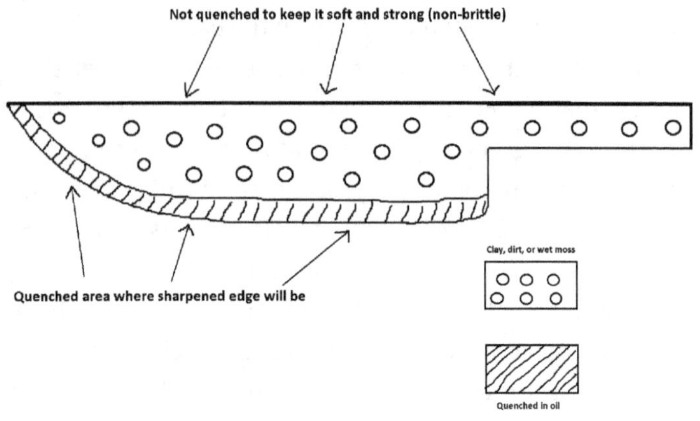

Quenching a Tool

The next topic I will discuss is called tempering. Now believe it or not, the tempering process is just a way to stabilize the steel molecules and it lowers the hardness, so that the metal is more workable and less brittle. This can be done by heating a steel to a constant 500 F for a couple of hours. Tempering is useful in many applications and tools, but for simplicity of the path of the empty hand, it is not necessary. If you only quench the striking or cutting edge of your tool as I described in the last section, It is an unnecessary step. I will teach you how to temper in case you want to take your blacksmithing to the next level though. Tempering can be done with an oven, toaster oven, or fire brick oven. Keep the fire or heat at a constant desired temperature of between 350 and 500 F. Place your steel inside the heat for over 2 hours. Let it cool and you have tempered steel.

Once you have created charcoal, annealed steel, hammered steel using a homemade forge, and quenched the steel, you can consider yourself a blacksmith of the empty-handed path. That is something to be proud of. Have fun with it.

This next section of the book will be what I refer to as "Odin's sunfire furnace". It is basically a sand heater that is powered by a homemade photo voltaic panel. The heater consists of a toaster element sitting inside a container filled with sand. Sand can hold heat for a very long time. It also has a very high melting point. We will be using a ceramic clay pot or crock pot to make it a type of radiant heater.

Take an old toaster apart. The part that glows red when turned on is the heating element. We take out one side of this element. Now we solder insulated wires to the element. We put several inches of sand in the bottom of our clay pot, crock pot, steel cooking pot, or whatever you choose for your radiant containment device. We now suspend the element over the pot with a piece of wood using the wires we just soldered. We want the element positioned in the pot deep enough to have at least 3-6" of sand above, below, and around the element. Now fill in the container with sand. Now wire your heating element to your AC power supply. It will take some time for the sand to heat up and radiate, but once its warm, it will stay warm for hours. If you use this hooked up to a solar panel, 12v battery, dc to ac inverter configuration, the power of the sun should give you enough electricity to keep a room warm for the majority of the day and night. You could also plug the toaster element wires into a power outlet if you chose to build the ac generator with rotating magnetic field and transformer build I explain in my chapter on lightning.

Sand Heater with toaster heating element

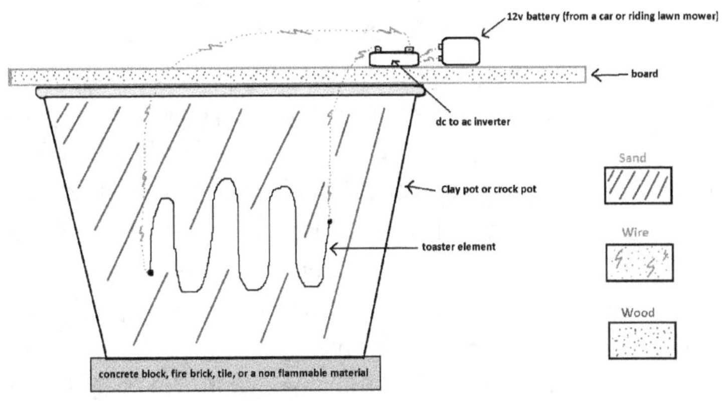

Sand Heater

This section will be about homemade wood burning stoves. We have been using fire as a way to heat and cook for thousands of years. Hopefully you are lucky enough to have a wood burning stove already installed in your home for emergencies. Following the path of the empty hand, I will show you several ways to create and install an emergency improvised wood burning stove.

At the most basic level, a wood burning stove is essentially a fire resistant container that holds a fire and exhausts the smoke and harmful chemicals and gases out. Certain materials hold heat better than others, and radiate heat better than others, but we will use what we have access to.

A list of possible items to use as your burn chamber are as follows, a steel barrel with a lid, a steel or metal trash can with a lid, a large and thick metal box or container, an empty propane canister, or fabricate one will steel scrap and weld it together. Use extreme caution if you decide to go with a propane canister or a container that had flammable and explosive chemicals inside it once. Make sure it has been completely emptied, fan out any left over vapors, and drill or cut them open outdoors. It would also be a good idea once you get them open to build a small fire inside them to burn out any residue that could have gotten into any cracks or imperfections in the metal.

After you have your burning chamber selected, you have to give it an access panel to add wood to your fire. You can either have the door on a hinge, or a sliding door in a track. Its really just a matter of preference and what you have on hand to use. You need to make sure it is airtight though. You don't want you and your family breathing carbon monoxide or smoke. This leads me to the third part of a homemade wood burning stove. The vent pipe for the exhaust.

Wood Stove with a through wall exhaust

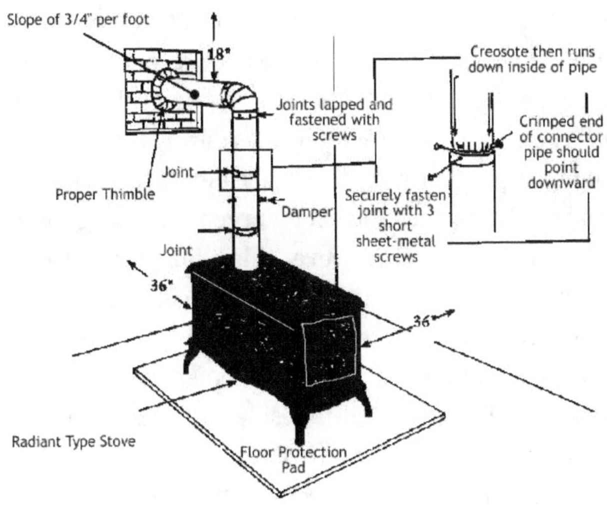

Wood Stove with a through window/wall exhaust

You can use sheet metal, steel pipe, old hvac metal pipes or even self fabricated rectangular tubing. Do be careful of some hvac metal duct work though. Many of them are galvanized metal, which is ok, but you have to start a fire outside and burn that zinc coating off of the pipes. It is a toxic fume and you will see green flames in your fire. Be sure to get the fire really hot and rotate and adjust your pipes every so often to get all of the zinc off. When the pipes cool off, scrub them with steel wool or a scrubber to clean them up on the outside. Now you have a good set of safe exhaust pipes.

Now that you have your stove assembled and ready to install, I will go over safety. How and where to place it, and I will explain venting methods. Keep in mind that this wood burning stove is just for extreme emergencies during the winter. People should have generators with a space heater, kerosene heaters, or propane heaters as normal emergency heating sources for winter power outages. However this book follows the path of the empty hand. We assume the worse scenarios, and fight to survive. Wood has worked for thousands of years, and it will always work. Although this is just for emergency I will make my recommendations as closely to residential fire code as I possibly can. Above all, stay safe and alive.

The wood burning stove needs to be at least 36" from any combustible material. You also need to have it placed on non combustible material like tile, brick, or stone. 36" x 36" from each outside edge. You can have your stove closer to walls, but you need special reflective materials and check with your local fire codes to see what is approved.(See later in this chapter for a highly heat resistant material made with cooking supplies called starlight.)

Venting of your wood burning stove is critical. The safest and best way to vent your emergency wood stove is to run it out of an opened window. This is my preferred method because you don't have to put any holes in your walls or roof. There will be less potential for water damage and it cuts down on fire risk using a window. If you would like a more permanent way, do some research on chimney tie ins and through wall venting. For our window exhaust system we will be cutting some sheet metal that is a perfect fit for our window opening. You can get this sheet metal from one side of a washing machine, clothes dryer, or stove. Whatever you can find. Cut out a hole in your sheet metal where your vent pipe will be going through. Make the hole slightly under sized so you have to force it in place and its air and water tight. We have to run the pipe out from the window about 6" then elbow it vertical going up a few feet. You will want it to still be under the roof overhang and several feet below it. Put sealant,glue, caulk, or starlight(ill explain starlight later in this chapter) all around your sheet metal inside and outside of your home to keep out the elements. If the weight of your exterior vent pipe is too much for your sheet metal, you can give it a stronger frame with some metal or pipe. You could also run a chain or wire from a roof overhang down to the elbow joint to help keep your outside elbow and pipe in place. Do what you have to do to get it safe, secure and working properly.

Only burn dried dead branches, twigs, river drift wood, and seasoned fire wood. Don't burn greenwood or construction timber. Start a fire and Enjoy!

A very special fire resistant material can be make out of baking and cooking ingredients found in most kitchens. It is similar to a material some refer to as starlight. It is used in aerospace ,metallurgy, and manufacturing because it can withstand over 7000 F. It is safe, non toxic, workable like play dough until it dries, and very fire resistant. The ingredients are flour, corn starch, powdered sugar, and baking soda. Two parts flour (40g), 1 part (20g) of everything else, and 25g of water.

Homemade Fire Resistant material that can withstand 7000 F

Flour - 40 grams
Corn Starch - 20 grams
Powdered Sugar - 20 grams
Baking Soda - 20 grams
Water - 25 grams

Combine all ingredients first dry with a fork inside of a bowl, then add water and mix the ingredients thoroughly until it reaches a doughy like substance.

Each ingredient serves a specific purpose. Flour is the binder and it holds everything together. Cornstarch reduces stickiness and helps it keep its shape. Powdered sugar is what creates a carbon foam to protect. Baking soda when heated, releases CO2 and water which inflates the carbon foam from the powdered sugar giving us a heat and flame resistant outer coating. Once burned, this carbon foam layer insulates the rest of the material from heat and flames. This material when mixed and made correctly should be able to withstand over 7000 degrees Fahrenheit. Empty-handed Odin thinks its yummy! Enjoy.

4

Wind

In this chapter I am going to teach you how Empty-handed Odin can harness the power of the wind. This is important because you may not be able to use the sun for photo voltaics in some regions, or there will only be a few hours of good sun at certain times. We will be following the path of the empty hand, so we will only be using salvaged parts to build the wind turbine generator. We will use a box fan or oscillating fan for the blades to catch the wind. We connect these blades to a rotating shaft that is connected to an ac generator, an alternator, or even a rotating magnetic field generator.

Wind Turbine

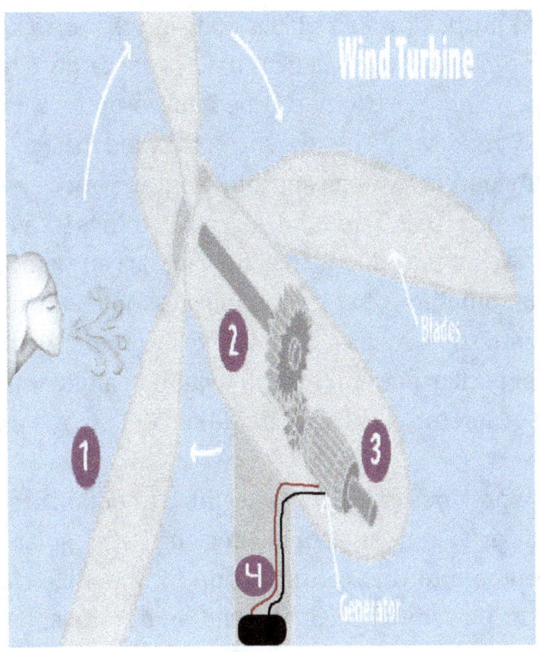

1. Use any balanced fan blade that you can find
2. Attach fan blade to a shaft with either a gear or fitting to hold a bike chain or serpentine belt.
3. Attach the fan blade shaft to an ac generator or vehicle alternator.
4. You hook your ac generator or alternator to a battery.

The wind pushes the fan blades, causing the shaft of the ac generator to turn, which causes the ac generator to manifest a voltage. This electricity can be hooked up to a battery, a capacitor, or a device. The strength of the wind that day, and the maximum output wattage and amperage of your ac generator will determine what items and how many things it can run.

The most simple build is the fan blade ac generator directly powering something, but if the wind dies for a bit, your device will shut off, so I have included plans to incorporate a battery to charge for backup power. This will require an alternator instead of an ac generator, a battery charge controller, and a dc to ac inverter.

See my previous chapters to see how to build these out of salvaged parts. You can actually hook up both a solar cell and wind turbine into this configuration for a double chance of getting the power you need. May the winds forever be in your favor.

5

Lightning

Empty-handed Odin can manifest lightning. Electricity can be manifested with the use of a rotating magnetic field. This is the basic explanation of an ac generator. In this chapter I will show several setups to achieve this using common household items.

The path of the empty hand means that we start with nothing, so I will first teach you how to make an improvised solder gun. We will use it to dis-assemble household items and salvage parts for generating electricity.

A solder gun or soldering iron is basically a heated piece of steel used to melt solder. Solder is basically a low melting conductive material. Think of it like glue that can carry electricity. The easiest, most basic soldering gun can be made with a paperclip, piece of wire, or a metal coat hanger. I personally prefer a medium copper wire as a solder gun because it can be used for soldering and solder reclaiming. Be sure to give it a handle so you don't burn your hands. The heat source will be a lighter, a candle, or a small fire.

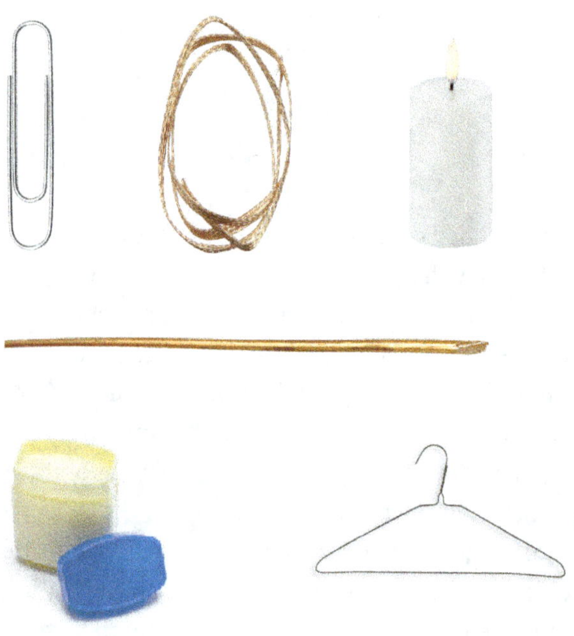

Makeshift Solder Items

We next need to find a flux so that we can reclaim some solder off of an old or unused circuit board so that we can make good connections on our improvised items. You could probably get by with just twisting wire connections, using electric tape, or wire nuts, but on the empty handed path, we have to assume you have nothing. The definition of flux is "the action or process of flowing". Flux makes the solder flow. A common household item that can be used as flux is petroleum jelly or Vaseline.

Another thing that might be useful is a "solder braid". It's basically something that will pull off solder in case you make a mistake or you want to salvage some solder for later. A solder braid is as simple as a few fine gauged copper wires braided together with petroleum jelly on it.

I will now teach you how to build what we can refer to as the "Empty-handed Odin Generator". It is a motor, magnets, a copper coil, a microwave transformer, and a surge protector. The motor needs to have a shaft so we can create a rotating magnetic field. There are three good sources. An ac generator, a motor out of the compressor of a refrigerator, and a motor out of a washing machine. There are many other sources but I am just going to cover these sources.

AC Generator

35

We need to use a pull start method on our motor to get everything going once fully assembled. This will be as simple as winding a string around the shaft many times, then pull the string causing the shaft to spin. On the tip of our motor shaft we have to attach two magnets. We can use speaker magnets. Keep in mind the heavier the magnets are and less aerodynamic these magnets are, the more drag and stress they will put on the motor. Keep it light and lean if possible, but the magnets should be at least the size of a silver dollar. On one side of the shaft we have the north pole of the magnet facing out, and on the other side we have the south pole facing out. We have to either glue, epoxy, caulk, or tape them to the shaft. The shaft will have pretty high rpm and will always be running so make sure they are on secure.

The snake coil and magnet assembly. To create the "snake coil" we find some thick copper wire. This can be found by stripping the insulation off of electric cords, pulling it out of electronic components, or off old copper windings of a non-working motor, transformer, or stater. Get something about the size of a soda can around. Leave about 6" of wire in the hand holding the can, and start winding the copper around the can. Once you have the area of the can wound, slide it down and repeat the process about three times or so. Also be sure to leave another 6" of slack on the other end for electrical connections. We will take the winding and shape it like an arch or rainbow with a speaker magnet on each end. We attach the coil to the magnets with glue, hot glue, or electric tape around the magnet end and first loop of wire.

Serpent Coil with Magnets

The microwave transformer is next. We use a transformer to step up the voltage in our machine. A note of caution when taking apart a microwave for parts, or any electronics. Capacitors can contain enough voltage and amperage to really hurt someone even if left unplugged for several years. Use rubber gloves,rubber or plastic handled tools, and be very careful. I always work on electric stuff one-handed so I don't complete a circuit with my body. Carefully open up the microwave, identify the transformer, cut the wires to get it loose and removed, then put the case back on the microwave for safety.

Microwave Transformer

Microwave Transformer

The next component of our generator is a surge protector. We use it to hook up our lights, fans, electronics, and anything else we need. I prefer a surge protector because it has a safety fuse switch that will power everything off if too much current is created. If you can't find a surge protector, an outlet socket would work. We will also be using another cut electric cord plug with wires. We run wires from the high voltage side of our transformer to the wires of our surge protector strip. We take the other cut electric plug I was talking about and use it to power our motor. This completes the circuit and allows our motor to continually run after our initial pull start.

Surge Protector

Surge Protector

We will now place our components together. When assembling and putting the motor beside the snake coil, we must have the motor shaft directly lined up and close proximity to our snake coil arch but not touching it.

We solder all wire connections together. We might need to scrape the ends of the wires for a clean electrical connection. Some wire has an enamel coating on it. After all joints are soldered, tape them with electric tape to ensure they don't come loose.

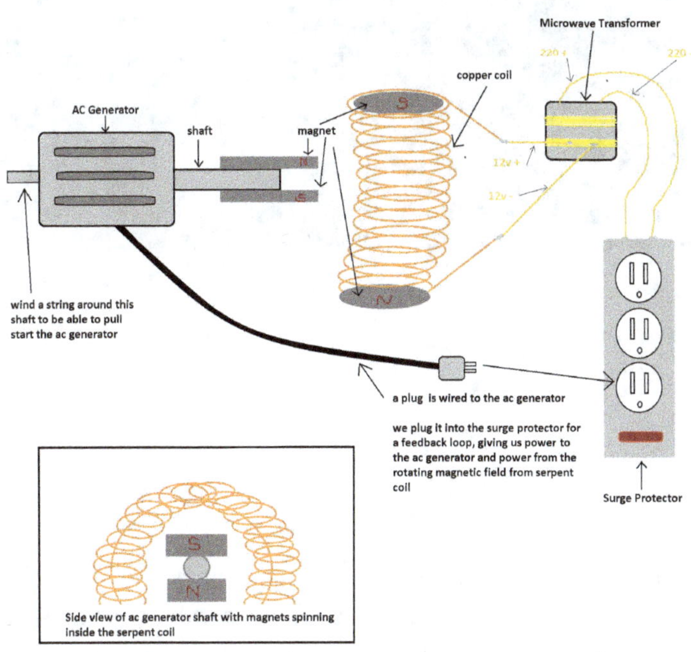

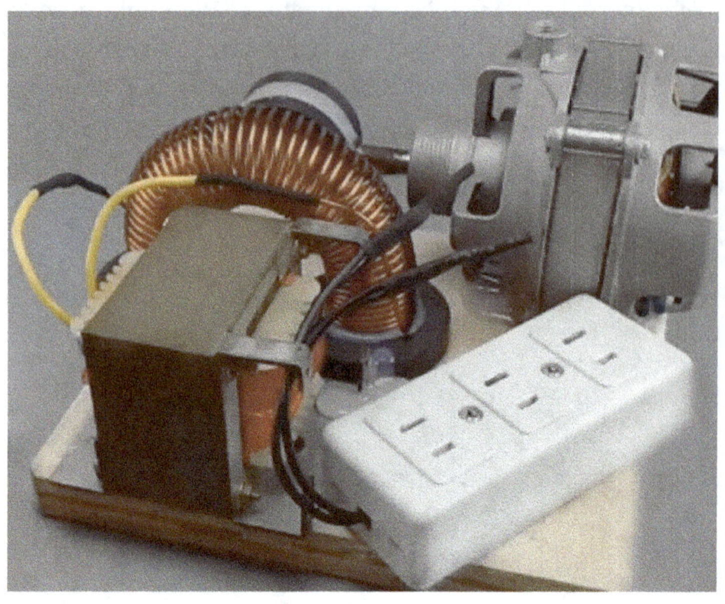

Empty-handed Odin's lawnmower lightning bolt. This device is simply an internal combustion engine combined with a car alternator or an ac generator. An ac generator is ideal for home power, but an alternator can be used if you change its dc power to ac with an inverter.

I will be showing how to add a small internal combustion engine to an alternator or ac generator to manifest energy.

The items I chose for these tasks include an engine from a lawnmower or a weed wacker. I chose a push mower engine and weed wacker because they will be the most common engines to find everywhere. We can find an electrical motor inside a refrigerator or washing machine, and the transformer and capacitor out of a microwave. We can use a 12v car battery or 12v riding lawnmower battery for storage. We will salvage parts from old electronics like a vcr, dvd player, tv, and video game systems. We will be using magnets out of car speakers, computer speakers, and home theater speakers. These designs are just for simple everyday power for lighting, fans, electronics,computers,video games, and light medical equipment. These designs aren't designed to run an air conditioning unit, a microwave, or a heater unless scaled up considerably. It may sound overwhelming at first, but I will keep it very basic, easy to understand, and as few parts as possible. I will also include good diagrams with descriptions.

We need the rotating shafts of the engine and the ac generator/alternator connected. For this task we will use a serpentine belt or bicycle chain. The belt has to be tight with no slack. Basically you are using the power of an internal combustion engine to turn its shaft which turns the belt, which then turns the shaft of the ac generator, which then generates a voltage. You can run the output wires of your ac generator to a surge protector plug. You can hook your devices up to this surge protector. The engine will have to be exhausted or just run it outdoors. I recommend outdoors but protected from the elements. Use plastic conduit or pvc pipe to protect the wires from your ac generator outdoors that lead to your surge protector indoors.

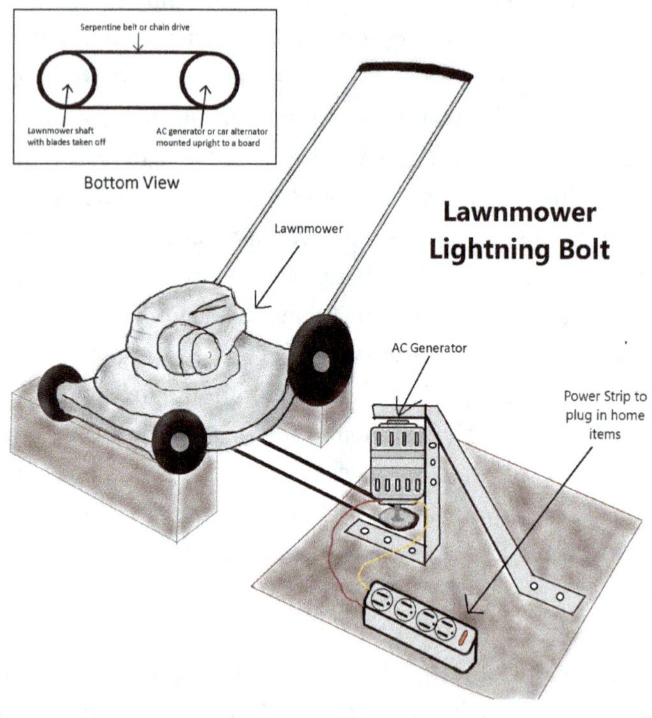

If you want to run your household items with either a solar panel or an engine with a car's alternator, you will have to change the power from direct current (dc) to alternating current (ac) for household appliances. There are a lot of cheap inverters available. They look like a surge protector with plug in outlets and the end connection will have either a car cigarette lighter plug, or battery terminal wires, or both. I hope you are lucky enough to have one of these, or be able to trade for one, but keeping with the path of the empty hand, we will be using salvaged parts we can find to build one for ourselves. The setup will be exactly the same as the previous section, "engine with an ac generator", but the very end of the process is modified to incorporate an inverter.

Salvaged part 1000 watt dc to ac inverter is what we will be building for this. It will provide enough wattage to run several things at once. The parts needed for this is a microwave transformer, 16 transistors d718, a heatsink, a power strip, 330 ohm .25 watt resistor (qty 2), and a 1k ohm .25 watt resistor(qty 2).

Start by attaching your d718 transistors to your heatsink. 8 per row. (These transistors act as amplifiers for your electricity. Having less gives less wattage but adding more allows you to run more electronic devices. If you can only find 2 or more of these transistors that would be enough to power a couple small things. If you add more than 16 like in the configuration I'm showing, be sure to add them in even numbers and one on each side of the heat sink.) It is best to put thermal compound on the back of every transistor for better heat transference so your equipment lasts longer. If you can't find thermal compound, you can make some with a mixture of aluminum pop can powder and vaseline or petrolium jelly. (D718 is a TO-3P packaged NPN transistor made by many electronics components manufacturers. The transistor is designed to be used in high power audio amplifier applications and capable to deliver output audio of 45 to 50

Watts.)

Heat Sink

Heat SInk

Transistor / Mosfet

S = Source

G = Gate

D = Drain

Transistor / Mosfet

LIGHTNING

d718 Transistor

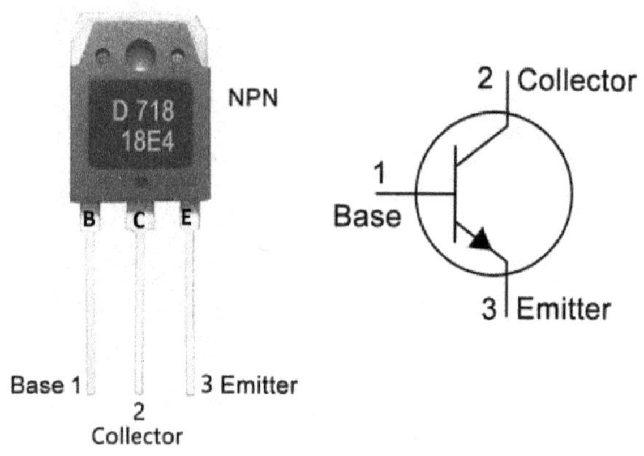

D718 Transistor

Resistor

Band A
1st Digit
Band B
2nd Digit
Band C
Multiplier
Band D
% Tolerance

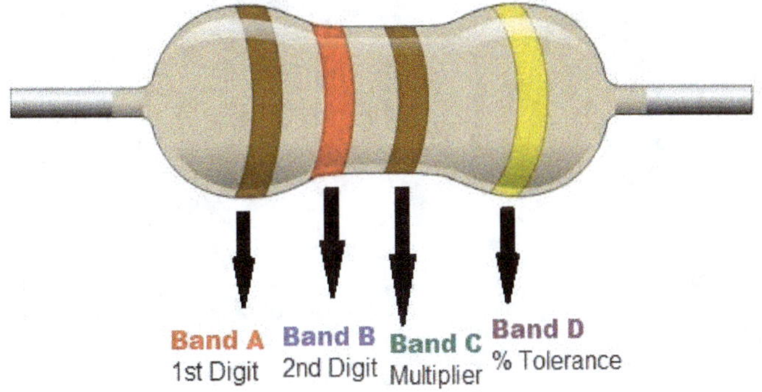

Diode

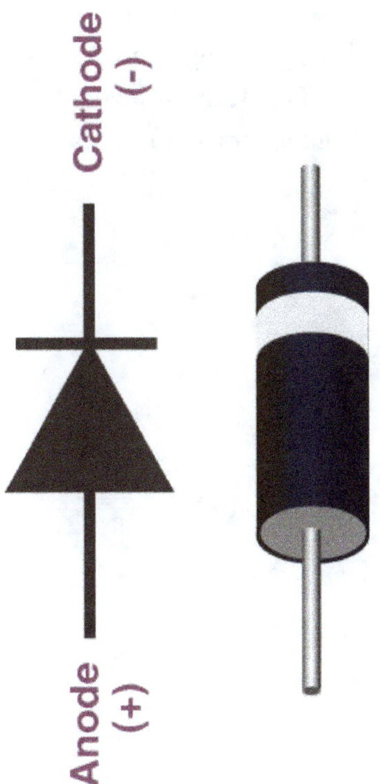

Now we wire the transistors together. We use a copper wire and connect in series 14 of the transistors on the emitter side of the transistor. We leave the far right transistor of each row out of this connection.

1000 Watt dc to ac Inverter Build

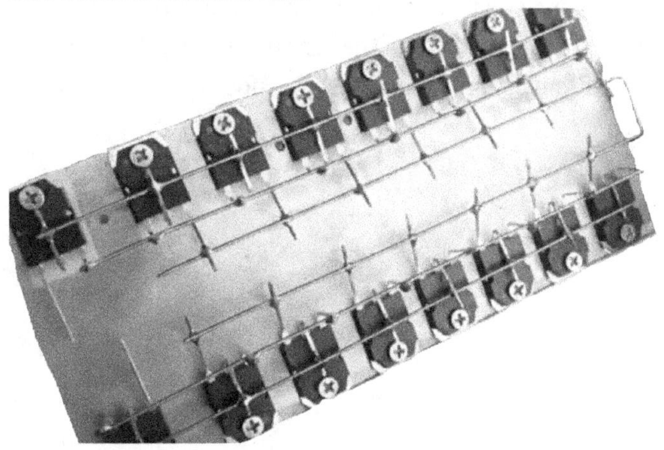

We now wire the collector pins in a series. We connect all 8 on the top row and all 8 on the bottom row. Next we connect the base connections. We connect all 8 base connections on the top row in a series with a piece of copper wire, and we all connect all 8 base connections on the lower row together in series.

We now connect a 330 ohm .25 watt resistor. On the silver band side of the resistor, we solder it on the emitter side connection series. We connect the other side of it to the transistor that doesn't have a connection to its base side yet.(remember how we left two resistors on outside edge empty earlier). Now we take another 330 ohm .25 watt resistor and connect it to the other row of transistors. We connect the resistor to the end transistor connecting the emitter to the base of the outside transistor. We have the silver ring facing the base side.

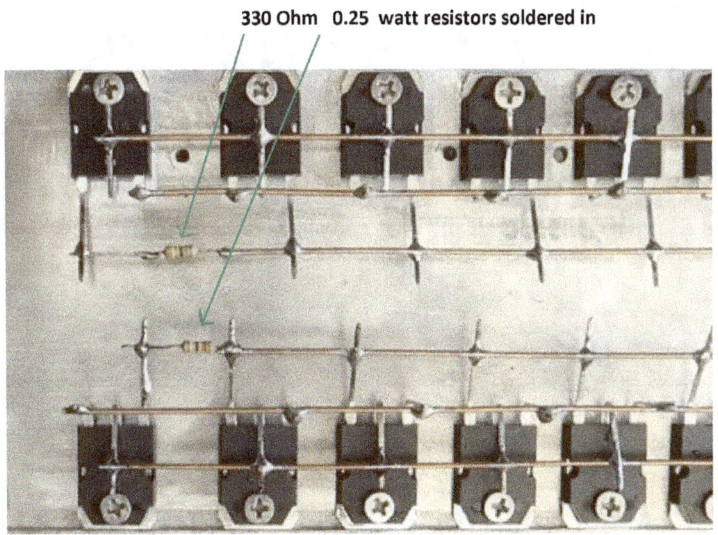

330 Ohm 0.25 watt Resistors Soldered in Place

We now take a 1k ohm .25 watt resistor and connect it to the collector side of the transistor we were just connecting to. The gold ban should be facing the transistor we just connected to. We then attach the other side of the resistor to the opposite side row, the transistor on the end of the base side.

1k ohm 0.25 watt Resistor Solder Points

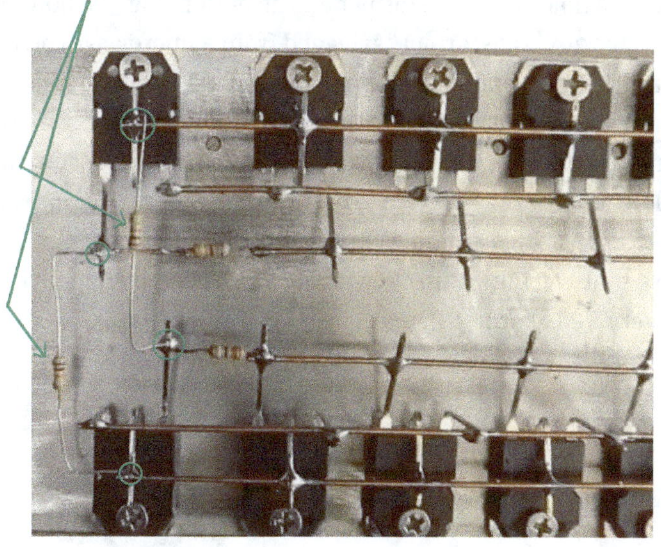

1k ohm 0.25 watt Resistor Solder Points

We now take another 1k ohm .25 watt resistor and attach it to
the base side of the small resistor to collector side of opposite

row transistor.

Now we put our fully soldered dc to ac inverter on a wooden board and attach it. Make sure it has enough room on the wooden board to hold your transformer and an outlet plug. We now put our 12v 220v transformer (salvaged from a microwave) on the board. We also put our power strip or electrical outlet onto the board. Next we connect the microwave transformer. One 12v wire from transformer goes to one side of the transistor collector side. The other 12v wire goes to the other row's collector side. We connect the 0v middle connection of the transformer to a wire that we will connect to a battery. Yellow is negative to battery, red goes to positive.

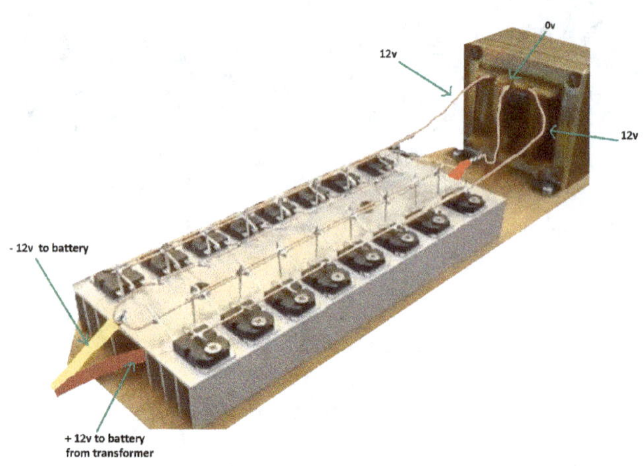

Inverter wired to Transformer and Battery Wires

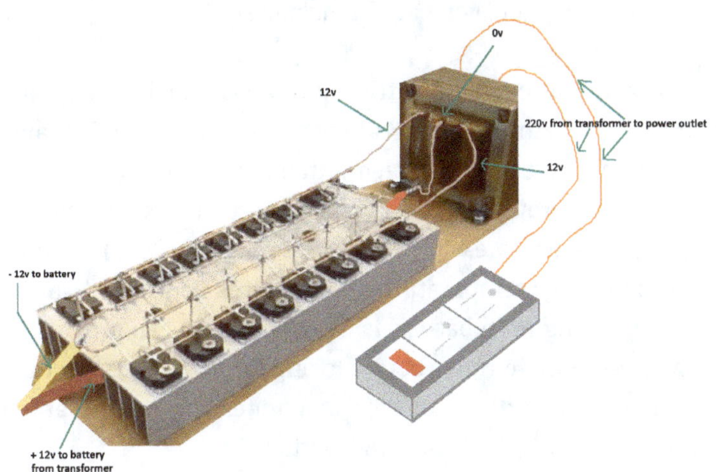

Inverter Wired to Microwave Transformer to Surge protector and Battery Wires

Now hookup your battery. Plug something in, and test it. If you suspect problems, go over all connections and make sure solder is solid at all points. Congratulations, you now have a working 1000 watt dc to ac inverter. This inverter can also be used in unison with either an internal combustion engine hooked up to an alternator to charge a battery, or even a solar panel hooked up to a battery, and you have home power. Enjoy.

I am going to explain a little more about car batteries and alternators in this section. Car batteries and most riding lawn mowers are 12v and can average 500 amps but after 30 seconds of use they can drop down to 7.2 volts per second. Reserve capacity is a measurement we will also use. Reserve capacity is measured in minutes at a temperature of 80 degrees Fahrenheit. If the reserve rating for a battery is 80, the battery can provide 25 amperes for 80 minutes before losing its power. So you could run 180 watts worth of stuff for 80 minutes off a battery, at full charge. 25 amp x 7.2 volts = 180 watts

Most standard car alternators have outputs starting around 60 amps and go up. I'll use the lowest to give us a baseline of what to expect. Alternators should put out around 13-14 volts while engine is idling. I will use 12v in the formula so we under clock our output. This will give us an idea of what we can run with this setup and how many watts to expect to use. 60 amp x 12v = 720 watts. This isn't a whole lot of power but it is plenty for your survival necessities. Also, like I said earlier, this configuration can be scaled up even to a massive scale if you had many engines and each engine setup had a group of big alternators all on a fly wheel assembly. Also, if gasoline isn't available or expensive, you can run these 2 cycle internal combustion engines on hydrogen gas. You will still need a little gasoline or something to lube the engine, but its a pretty easy modification. Just be careful.

Here are many electrical components we can use.

Motor,mosfets/transistors, heat sinks, capacitors, resistors, diodes, transformers, pumps, led's, fans, and magnets.

Refrigerator - transistors, capacitors, diodes, led's, motor, wiring, circuit boards, coolant pump, resistors

Washing Machine - water pump, motor, hoses, transistors, diodes, capacitors, copper wire, resistors, belt

Microwave - transformer, capacitor, magnatron, transistors, diodes, resistors, power supply, fan, light, copper wire, microwave shielding, turn table motor, circuit boards

Dryer - heating element, blower fan, motor, capacitor, transistor, diodes, resistors, wiring, circuit boards, a serpentine belt

VCR,Dvd player - lasers, transistor, capacitor, resistor, led's, small motor, wiring, circuit board

Video Game Systems - (don't be sacrilegious, only use broken and non working game systems for parts) circuit boards, transistors, capacitors, resistors, diodes, wiring, heat sinks, fan, power supply, laser,

TV - electric cords, circuit board, transistors, resistors, diodes, heat sinks, speakers, magnets, led's, and the older tv's will have a mini transformer, copper wire, and uhf/vhf components.

Computers - Ac power supply with fan, heat sinks, transistors, resistors, diodes, cd drive motor, laser, wiring, and circuit boards.

Speakers - magnets, wiring,

Washing Machine Motor

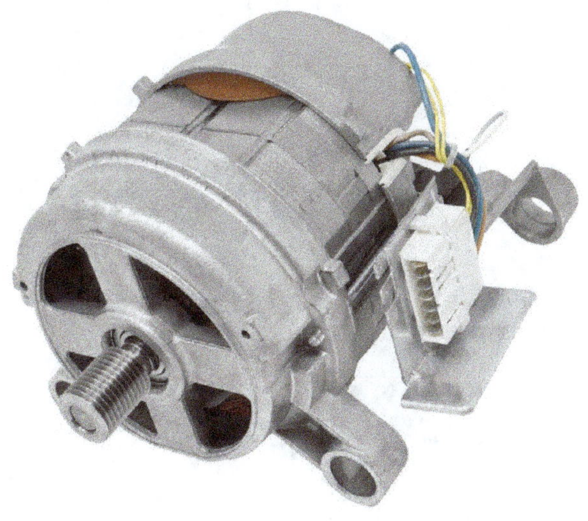

Refridgerator Compressor

There is a motor inside this cannister which can also be re-magnetized to function as an ac generator

There are many more sources for the components you might be hunting for, but this list is pretty common household items and will cover the major items you need.

A final word of advice, Start yourself a salvage pile of old appliances and electronics. Don't throw them in the trash anymore. Dedicate a cabinet or closet, or a shed or section of your garage to your salvage pile. Keep them in water resistant containers or bags. Best to put your salvaged items in a simple faraday cage. Even if something doesn't work, there will still be a lot of useful items inside. We are currently a throw away society because stuff is so readily available and cheap. When something breaks we throw it away and buy a new one, but one day things might cost a lot more, or we may cut down trading with certain manufacturing places,which would make some items very hard to find. If we don't start producing these items locally, we will all wish we had saved all the electronic and appliance "junk" over the years which could actually become priceless treasures under that scenario. When you understand the manufacturing process from digging minerals out of the ground all the way to the finished product, you will appreciate the true value of all the things that most of us take for granted every day. So .... Save, Salvage, and Share.

6

Thunder

In this chapter I will explain how to make your own photo voltaic solar panels. I will also show how to make a battery charge controller out of salvage parts and show how you can weld with a 12v car battery.

Solar photovoltaic (PV) cells harness the power of the sun. The light gets turned into an electric current. Following the path of the empty hand, I will show how to make a solar panel out of old cd's and dvd's. This is something very commonly found in most homes and vehicles. We will also be using copper wire to wind the cd's and using it for our connections. I recommend wire gauge or thickness to be around 22 gauge, which is around .025" thick. You will be able to find this on many salvaged parts as windings. It can be bigger or smaller, just use what you can find. We will be using 24 cd's or dvd's. The reflective non printed side is what we want up and facing the sun. Use a drill bit, or red hot nail and put 2 holes in each cd about a half inch from the outside edge, and have the gap between the holes about 1". We leave about 4" loose wire going through one hole, wrapping through center hole to outside edge. We wrap the cd 46 times. On the last winding which would be number 46, we put the wire through the other hole and leave about 4" loose. We repeat this process until all 24 cd's have been wound 46 times each.

CD Wound 46 times with + and - terminals

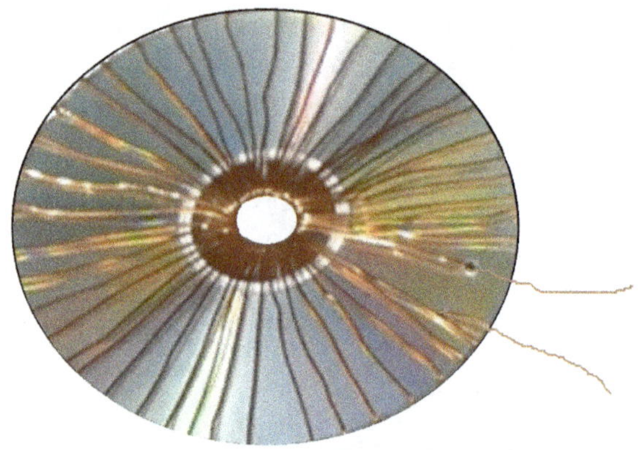

CD Wound With Copper Wire 46 Times

Next step is to place the 24 cd's on a piece of wood that has a lip all around it, or a plastic tote lid. Lay them out in a 4 x 6 rectangular pattern. Make sure the reflective side of the cd's are facing up toward the sun. We now wire the cd's in a series. We solder each connection for a good connection. On our end wires from cd #1 and cd #24, we attach and solder a heavier gauge insulated wire. These 2 wires are what we will connect to a battery or the device we choose to power. Our windings and connections are now complete. Make sure no wires that aren't supposed to be touching are not. Now plug the 2 wires up to a small l.e.d. or a low voltage device to make sure that your solar panel is fully functional before we encase it. Now we will encase or cover our photovoltaic panel for protection from water and moving around. The important part is it needs to keep out water, and sunlight has to be able to pass through it. You could use a clear epoxy, clear caulk, polyurethane, clear coat, or clear rubberized paint. If you can't find anything like that, put a clear piece of plastic over it and ensure a water tight seal. You could use vaseline, petroleum jelly around the edge to seal the plastic.

24 CD's wired in series for a 220v solar panel

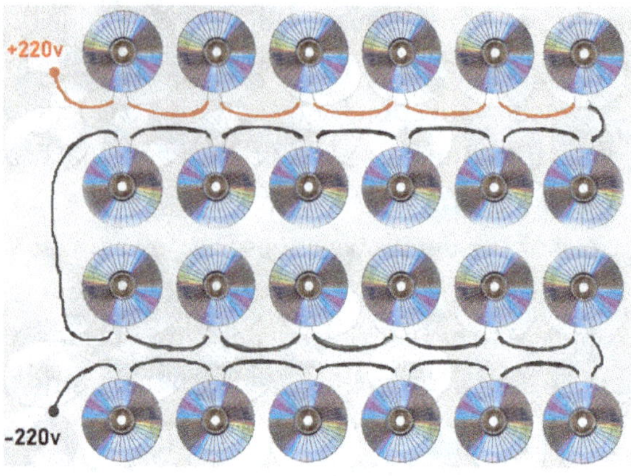

We now have a working and water resistant solar panel. Since the 24 cd's are wired in a series, we will have around 220v dc power. We can now hook up stuff we need powered, or connect it to a 12v car battery to recharge it. You could create several of these panels and should be able to maintain a decent amount of energy in a battery for emergency needs.

One important thing you need to know is that after the sun goes down, the electricity stored in your battery can travel back to your solar panel causing you to lose all the power you just added. You have to either disconnect the wires to your battery manually before sun goes down, which is the easiest way for beginners, or have a battery charge controller connected in between your solar panels and battery. It's pretty easy to hook up your battery at sunrise, and disconnect before sunset. For those that would like to take this setup to the next level, I will teach you how to make a very basic battery charge controller from salvaged parts.

A battery charge controller is a circuit that only allows the electricity to flow in one direction. We need this if we want to be hands free, low maintenance and minimal time working with our solar panels and battery. The battery charge controller we will be building is for a 12v car or riding lawn mower battery. It requires 5 main components that we have to salvage. You can get these components out of old video game systems, vcr's, tv's, dvd players, appliances, and many various electronics. You just have to open stuff up and look inside. I will show a picture of all parts used in the build.

Battery Charge Controller

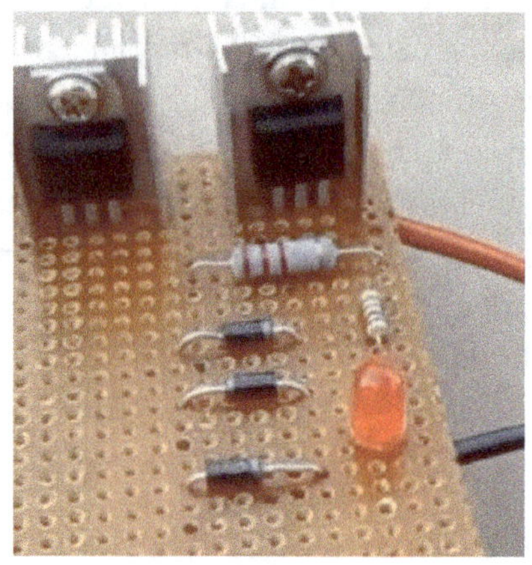

-2qty mosfets   7812 ic (L7812cv)

- 3qty diode   1N4007

- 1qty 2.2k resistance

- 1qty 3v Led

- 1qty 1k resistance

- 2qty heat sinks to hook the mosfets

- 1 hole board just to put it all together, could use wood and hot glue, or variants

Lets assume you have all of the parts salvaged and ready. First attach each mosfet to a heat sink. Use a thermal compound in between them. If you have to make your own thermal paste, use pop can shavings (aluminum powder) mixed into vaseline. Thermal compound helps with heat transfer to the heat sink. This will extend the life of your parts because they wont get too hot and melt.

Next we will wire our mosfets together. Solder a wire connecting the inputs together. Then solder a wire connecting the outputs together. Then connect the two grounds together with a piece of non insulated copper wire. Now we connect our 2.2k resistor. One side of the resistor connects to the output connection. The other side is connected to the ground wire. The silver or gold band side of the resistor is what is connected to the output connection. We will now attach the diodes. Lining up the silver bands on the end, we alternate them. We wire the diodes in a series as shown above.

The wire on the opposite side of our diode series is attached to the input of our battery. We connect a wire from our combined mosfet output and resistor going to battery.

Now we attach our l.e.d. so we know when it is working. We connect one end of the led to our connection where the diode series connects to the input wire that will go to the battery. The other side of led we connect to our little resistor that is 1k. Connect them at the color banded side of resistor. Now on the silver band side of the 1k resistor, connect it to the mosfet output connection.

Now we connect our solar panel wires to our homemade battery charge controller. First we connect our input to our mosfet bridged input spot. Now we connect the other solar panel wire to our spot that has the input wire going to the battery and the led connection.

Now we can connect our battery and we have a functioning solar panel, battery charge controller, and a battery getting charged up. Congratulations!

On the path of the empty hand, we might have to do some welding and fabricating. I am going to show you how to weld with a 12v car battery. You just need a charged battery, a pair of jumper cables, a welding rod or metal of similar type that you will be welding. Put your welding rod inside the black negative (-) jumper cable. Connect the red positive (+) to the metal part you will be welding. The power of the electricity will cause arcing and heat allowing you to melt the pieces and fuse them together. Caution. Starring at weld arcs can damage your eyes if unprotected, and electricity can electrocute and burn you. Proceed with caution. Also, if you are using a vehicle battery, be sure to disconnect all wires and remove the battery before welding. Wear a welding mask or very very strong sunglasses if no other option. If you don't have a welding mask with a lens, I recommend looking away while you do what is referred to "tack welding" You heat the metals in one spot or short beads until it is bonded. This should get you by in most instances, but don't expect any structural strength with heavy weight loads on the weld. Also only weld in 30 second intervals and take a break in between. This will keep your battery pushing maximum amperage for hotter welds. Welding can take some practice to make good bonds, but it can be very fun. Have fun and stay safe.

A simple Faraday cage can be made to store and protect your extra electronics and infrastructure items. A Faraday cage is basically just something that can block electro- magnetic fields.

This could be useful during very strong electrical storms and solar storms. It happens when a coronal mass ejection from the sun collides with the earth's magneto sphere. If the storm is very strong, It could cause power outages and fry electronics. Having a Faraday cage with a stash of electronic goodies can help you get through the transition time of a black out while waiting for power companies to fix everything.

A very simple cage can be made with cardboard, plastic, aluminum foil or mylar, and chicken wire or welded wire fencing. First put your items inside a cardboard box. Tape all the seams. Put your box inside a heavy duty trash bag. Then put your box inside a plastic tote with a lid. Now wrap your tote completely with aluminum foil or mylar. Make sure every area is covered, and a few layers is even better. I personally use mylar instead of aluminum foil. Mylar can be found in department stores in the camping section. They call it an "emergency blanket". Mylar is stronger, holds up better, and also helps block more emf radiation including microwaves. Once you have your tote wrapped really good with foil or mylar, get your metal welded wire fencing or chicken wire. I use a layer of both but ideally the smaller the gap in the wire, the better you achieve attenuation on the outer layer. Place your wire on the ground. Now place another piece of wire on the ground going the opposite direction. Place your tote in the center of the wire. Now pull the ends up of your wire just as if you were wrapping yourself a present with chicken wire. Overlap the wire over the top of the tote and secure it with a few pieces of loose wire. Now take another piece of chicken wire and wrap around the sides of the tote going all around the tote. Secure the piece with loose wire. You now have a Faraday cage.

Faraday Cage Parts List

I will explain what each layer does. The cardboard, trash bag, and plastic tote are all non conductive insulators. That means electricity won't pass through them. The tote also helps protect your items from moisture and pests. The aluminum foil and mylar are conductive, but electro-magnetic radiation blockers. The chicken wire and welded wire fencing are to achieve attenuation from electricity and electro-magnetic frequency. It reduces the amplitude and current strength. This will keep the electricity and emr from reaching your items. This is just a simple, path of the empty handed Odin method to have a faraday cage with items that most people would have in their home. It is very effective for its simplicity and cost. If this subject interests you, there is a lot of good information, websites, and books on the subject if you would like to take things to the next level.

Some items that I recommend having in a Faraday cage would be a generator. Some ac generators, alternators, motors, battery charge controllers, dc to ac power inverters, multimeters, power tools, transistors, resistors, radios, laptop computers, and anything else electronic that you personally enjoy or things that might entertain you. I also recommend keeping your salvaged electronics for parts inside their own faraday cage.

Embrace the path of the empty-hand and be thunderous.

7

The Empty-handed Odin Games

This book also brings us a new science and engineering competition called the "Empty-handed Odin" games. People get together and test their knowledge and skill by building stuff out of salvage parts in a timed, friendly, competition. This competition can be held in schools, college technical schools and science departments especially. It can be held in factories with maintenance people, engineering companies, manufacturing companies, and even at local science and tech fairs. One day it can be sort of like the "world series" or Olympics of science and engineering. It will bring invention, innovation, and bring science to a popular competitive level that humans enjoy.

Back of Book Cover

Empty-handed Odin wields the power of the gods within him. He is lightning, thunder, fire, rain, and wind incarnate. All these nature powers can be manifested through him into this physical dimension by channeling the knowledge and understanding of these forces from his mind, through his body, and out of his empty hands. He is pure power potential, manifested in its human form.

This book is about the path of the empty-hand. Primitive survival skills for the modern world. I will teach you how to manifest electricity from the sun, wind, and magnets without any starting tools or supplies. I will also teach you about water filtration and blacksmithing without any tools to start with. After reading this book you will be able to walk into any house with empty hands, and manifest electricity, clean water, and fire for infrastructure survival. This book is tailored for the average person with no prior knowledge, skills, tools, preps, or equipment, that may find themselves in a natural disaster survival situation. This book will help you build things for survival and have a higher quality of life while waiting for utility companies to get everything working again. This book also brings us a new science and engineering competition called the "Empty-handed Odin" games. People get together and test their knowledge and skill by building stuff out of salvage parts in a timed, friendly, competition.

www.ingramcontent.com/pod-product-compliance
Lightning Source LLC
Chambersburg PA
CBHW061250140726
47998CB00006B/2175